CALL HIM
FATHER NATURE

"I found this book to be an entertaining, well-written
biography for 8-12 year olds. The story of John Muir's life
deserves re-telling, with all its adventure and spirited love
of nature."

> —Harold Wood, Coordinator, Sierra Club
> John Muir Education Project

"Fascinating, and easy to read."

> —Bertha A. Daubendiek, Executive Secretary and
> founder in 1952 of the Michigan Nature Association

JOHN MUIR
photo provided by the National Park Service

CALL HIM
FATHER NATURE

The Story of John Muir

PATRICIA TOPP

BLUE DOLPHIN

Published by Blue Dolphin Publishing, Inc.
P.O. Box 8, Nevada City, CA 95959
Web: www.bluedolphinpublishing.com
Orders: 1-800-643-0765

ISBN: 1-57733-047-1

Library of Congress Cataloging-in-Publication Data

Topp, Patricia, 1923–
    Call him Father Nature : the story of John Muir / Patricia Topp.
        p. cm.
    Summary: A biography of the naturalist, founder of the Sierra
Club, and advisor to presidents on protecting western lands from
development.
    ISBN 1-57733-047-1
    1. Muir, John, 1838-1914—Juvenile literature. 2. Naturalists—
United States—Biography—Juvenile literature. 3. Conservation-
ists—United States—Biography—Juvenile literature. [1. Muir,
John, 1838-1914. 2. Naturalists. 3. Conservationists.] I. Title.

QH31.M9 T67 2000
333.7'2'092—dc21
[B]   00-023586

Cover concept: Lauren Zimmerman
Cover design: Jeff Case

Illustrations: © 2001 www.arttoday.com
Photos of John Muir are used with permission of the
National Park Service, John Muir National Historic Site,
4202 Alhambra Ave., Martinez, CA 94533

Printed in the United States of America

10   9   8   7   6   5   4   3   2   1

This book is dedicated to
Margaret Linsdeau,
my long-time friend,
who cared as passionately about animals
as John Muir cared about the forests.

Table of Contents

CALL HIM
FATHER NATURE

1

Will a Whipping Make You Learn?

The boys in the little school in Scotland chanted, "*Couldst, wouldst, shouldst.*" "*Amo, amas, amat,*" and "*Je va, tu vais, il va.*" The English, Latin, and French verbs were to be memorized like poetry.

Mr. Lyon, their teacher, said firmly, "Whipping improves a boy's memory." And he demonstrated his opinion on any poor pupil whose recital was less than perfect.

Three languages and spelling, arithmetic, history, and geography besides, and

that's not all. Then I have to go home and memorize Bible verses for Father, thought eight-year-old John. He was feeling sorry for himself. He dreamed of roaming the fields and the seashore, of climbing among the ruins of Castle Dunbar.

"Dreaming of the fields are ye, John?" Down came the rod on his fingers. Mr. Lyon had caught him out again. John bit his lip. He must keep a stiff face else the boys would mock him out on the playground. If he so much as whimpered, he'd have to challenge each boy to a fight to prove himself.

Next recess, John was roughest of all
when they played the switch game. The boys
made whips out of braided weed stems and
switched one another's legs. The one who
gave up first from the pain lost the game.

The boys tried to take Mr. Lyon's blows
and the punishment they gave one another
without flinching. "I'm Robert the Bruce,
King of Davel Hill," one would crow. The
others would try to drag him down from the
hill. Each boy's ambition was to be the best
fighter. Each wanted to go for a soldier when
he grew up. They looked on the thrashings
and battles as part of their training.

John would not have dreamed of skipping
school, but he escaped from the yard each
Saturday in spite of his father's warnings and
his beatings. "Ye will not be leaving the yard
the day. It's learning bad thoughts and bad
words from yon vagabonds, ye are." Father, a
strict Scotsman, was certain that bad boys
were to be punished in the world hereafter.
He made sure that they were punished in this
one. But Nature called, and John answered.

On their Saturday wanderings, the grammar school boys scoured the beach for shells. They watched eels, crabs, and other odd creatures of the tide pools. Sometimes they swam in these pools, after they had poked in a stick to check for boy-eating monsters. They ran great distances, jumped, wrestled, and climbed.

Often the boys played in the ruins of the 1000-year-old Castle Dunbar. One day they were playing prisoner's base at the castle. Some boys from a neighboring school appeared.

John challenged one of them, "What are ye staring at then, Robert?"

Robert replied, "I'll look where I have a mind to look. Just keep me from it. I dare ye."

"I'll soon let ye see whether I dare or no!" yelled John, and he gave Robert a right to the face. It took this little to start a grand fight.

When they were all sore and weary, they made peace. No great harm was done, except for a few bruises. But one of John's blue eyes was now black and blue.

"You're going to catch it, John. You can't hide that shiner."

And sure enough, Father have him another thrashing when he got home. "Gude boys are to stay and play in the yard. Gude boys are not to fight."

"It's not fair," John grumbled to his younger brother, Davie, when they were safely in their bed. "Father can thrash us for our own good. Mr. Lyon can thrash us for our own good. But when we just want to thrash one another, they punish us again."

This harsh upbringing made John Muir into a sturdy boy. Perhaps the thrashings did help his memory. But the repeated whippings did not keep him from the fields and woods. Those stolen Saturdays were the beginnings of John's wilderness wanderings.

2

Off for the New World

When John was about eleven years old, he read in his schoolbooks about an American bald eagle which robbed a fish hawk of its prey. He read Audubon's story of the flocks of passenger pigeons, which flew in such millions that they turned the sky dark. America's sugar trees and gold-filled streams crowded John's dreams.

One evening when John and Davie were studying at Grandfather Gilrye's fireside, Father came in with glorious news. "Bairns," he said, "ye need not learn lessons this nicht for we're starting for America the morn."

No more books! At first John and Davie were speechless with joy. But not for long.

"I'll . . . I'll find an eagle's nest!" John cried.

"A sugar tree!" exclaimed Davie.

"Have a passenger pigeon for a pet!"

"And get gold!"

Suddenly they thought of Grandfather whose family would be leaving him in his old age.

"We'll send you a big box of maple sugar," John promised.

"And it packed in gold," added Davie.

Grandfather looked solemn. He warned in a troubled voice, "Ah, poor laddies, you'll find something else ower the sea but sugar and gold and freedom from lessons. You'll find plenty of harrd, harrd work."

He gave each of the boys a gold coin for a keepsake.

That evening John boasted to his school-mates, "I'm for America the morn." And when they didn't believe him, "Just see if I am in school the morn."

Even parting from Grandmother and Grandfather Gilrye, from Mother and the sisters and brothers who were to come later, did not damp down the boys' joy for long.

Father and the boys, and their thirteen-year-old sister, Sarah, left Dunbar on the train for Glasgow. They departed from Scotland on a sailing ship. No sign of land did they see again for six weeks and three days.

It didn't seem a long time for John and Davie. No matter how rough the seas, they stayed on deck. No seasickness troubled them.

The sailors taught them to sing, "The Youthful Sailor Frank and Bold." They learned to heave on a rope to the rhythm of the sailors' work chanteys. When a sailor commanded, "Haul away on that line now," they hauled away with a will.

The captain asked John and Davie into his cabin. He gave them books to read and was astonished that Scottish boys would know so much Latin and French. They surprised him again by reading parts of his Bible with perfect English accents.

The friendly sailors pointed out sea creatures to the boys. They spied whales, sea-birds, dolphins. . . . "Why, I mind one time a dolphin saved the captain's life, . . ." one sailor would begin. And they would be off on another wild yarn to fascinate the wide-eyed boys.

Meanwhile, Daniel Muir was listening to the other emigrants, "The woods in Canada are so thick a man could use up his life clearing them." And, "Most of the wheat comes from Wisconsin." Father decided on Wisconsin.

They landed in America, but the trip didn't end at the coast. They traveled up the waterways, finally unloading at Milwaukee on Lake Michigan. Mr. Muir hired a farmer for $30 to haul their goods one hundred miles to Kingston. The farmer did not know that John's Father had brought along a set of scales that weighed about four hundred pounds. He had also brought a cast iron stove and all the provisions for any wilderness emergency.

The wagon sank again and again into the deep spring mud. "Never again," grumbled the poor farmer, "Never again, even for $100, will I haul such a load. Break my wagon, break my horse, break my heart!"

Sarah and the boys had been left in a rented room in Kingston while Mr. Muir went with a land agent to spy out the land. He returned with a neighbor, Mr. Gray, who hauled the Muir family and the remainder of their goods ten miles to where John's father had found land. There they built a shanty in a sunny, open glade in the woods above a lake edged with white water lilies.

John and Davie were more interested in a blue jay's nest that they had found than in their new home. Already they felt at home in the Wisconsin wilderness.

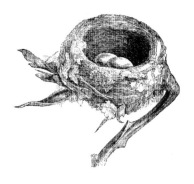

3

To Kill or Not to Kill?

John and Davie learned nature's lessons without books, without thrashings. The day after their arrival, they had found that, in some mysterious way, the jays had moved their eggs. They searched the woods.

"What's making that rapping sound?" Davie asked.

"Sh!" cautioned John, "See that dead tree, the one with the little circles in the bark. It must be some kind of woodpecker."

"Listen, there's a bird scolding."

"That will mean a hawk around some-where," John said.

Sure enough, they soon sighted a little kingbird chattering angrily at a large hawk. It

13

dived and dived again, pecking at the back of the hawk's head. The hawk flew clumsily, and the kingbird pestered it until it was out of sight.

The children saw many things in this new land that were new to them.

One warm night John saw sparkling lights. He said, "Davie, I'm seeing stars like someone hit me in the eye. Do you see anything strange?"

"Lots of fire-sparks in the meadow," Davie answered. "Maybe the Yankee can tell us what they are."

The "Yankee" was Mr. Muir's hired man. The boys often went to him to ask about things in nature that puzzled them.

"Oh, them ain't nothing but lightning bugs," the Yankee explained. "Get a cup, and we'll gather some."

They filled the cup with the sparkly little beetles and took them into the dark shanty.

"Look, they flash on and off," said Davie.

John marveled at the fireflies' soft glow.

Another time that they asked for the Yankee's help was when they heard from the woods a drumming sound. "Could it be a woodland bogie or a fairy?" Davie asked him.

"Come, I'll show you," the Yankee said. He led them to a small clearing. "Quietly now." He parted the bushes, and they saw a plump brown partridge drumming his mating dance.

When John was young, the passenger pigeon was not yet extinct. "Oh, what a bonnie bird!" Mr. Muir exclaimed when he first saw the rainbow colored feathers of the large pigeon. Even at that time, their flocks streaming north covered the sky, horizon to horizon, from dawn to sunset. Despite their beauty, every pioneer's gun was out. Pigeon pies were delicious. Farmers even destroyed the birds' roosts and killed the young birds to feed their pigs. They had no notion that ruining nesting places could, in time, make the species extinct.

The farmers also encouraged the neighborhood boys in a cruel and bloody game. The boys would choose teams to go killing birds and small mammals. The team with the highest head count won. The farmers felt that enemies to their crops were being killed. Later, when the farmers found out that the birds were their insect-killing friends, they stopped the killing.

John did not join in these bloody sports, but he was fond of shooting. One day he and

Davie and two Scotch boys their age were hunting blackbirds. Suddenly, a red-headed woodpecker flew up from the corn field.

"Shoot him; he eats corn," the Scotch boys yelled.

The woodpecker flew into the top of a white oak. John fired up, and the bird fell at his feet. "What beautiful feathers," John said. "Poor birdy, he's no dead yet. I'll have to put him out of his pain."

"Wring his neck," one of the boys advised.

"Bang him on the tree," Davie said.

John tried both, but to their astonishment, the bird gave a cry of alarm and flew up into the same tree. He adjusted his disordered feathers and began scolding at the boys.

"Yea! What a brave, bonnie bird." They cheered him and had no more thoughts about killing this particular corn-robber.

There were many ducks in the Wisconsin rivers and ponds. The settlers often feasted on them. One year Mr. Muir shot that most beautiful of all ducks, a wood duck. "Come bairns," he called, "admire God's handiwork. Just look at the colors of the feathers and how they shine." But despite its beauty, he had killed it.

It was every boy's ambition to shoot a Canada Goose. These were cautious birds and hard to shoot. One year John got a lucky shot and wounded a goose. The goose cried in terror, and the leader of the flock came circling back. The immense bird struck at John with its great wings. His gun was out of reach, so he covered his head the best he could with his arms.

Before he slept that night, John thought about this strange adventure. *How could it be that a mere bird was so noble as to risk its life for a companion? Did birds have minds and souls?*

4

Plenty of Harrd, Harrd Work

The boys were given two holidays a year,
the 4th of July and the first of January. They
could roam the woods and fields short times
on Sunday, before and after chores, Bible
lessons, Sunday school, and church service.
Sometimes, in the early evening, they were
allowed to fish or float on the pond in their
homemade boat. But Grandfather Gilrye had
been right. The boys found hard, hard work
in America.

Father set to work to build a house at Fountain Lake Farm. The rest of the family joined them in the fall of 1849.

Meanwhile, the boys had been put to work clearing brush from the land. They piled the brush and made immense bonfires. Once his father said to John, "Imagine how it would feel to be thrown into that fire. Think then that hellfire is many times hotter. All bad boys and sinners will be cast into fire in the hereafter just as we are casting in these branches, their suffering never to end."

John's heart was too full of faith and hope to take that terrible lesson seriously.

John plowed the fields when he was so small that his head barely came above the plow handles. At first they plowed around the tree stumps. Then John was put to work to

chop and dig out the stumps. He made the job harder on himself by trying to outwork the hired men.

It seemed in Father's nature to do all things the way that was hardest on their bodies. One day a Yankee, who stayed overnight at the Muir's, said to Mr. Muir, "Should wait till winter to husk the corn. More time then. Let the stalks stand. Cattle can trample them in come spring. Plow them under then."

Father thought it over. He decided it was a good idea. Instead of glorious Indian summer days to do the husking, they worked in zero temperatures. They got many a frosted finger.

The chores never ended.

"John, split the rails for the zigzag fence today."

"Sarah, fetch Mother more water."

"David, the kitchen garden wants hoeing."

"Daniel, the woodbox needs filling."

The hardest work was during harvest time. Work days were often seventeen hours long. John swung the cradle to cut the wheat. All of the family worked to rake it, bind it into sheaves, and thresh the kernels from the stalks. John even worked through a case of the mumps. Father said, "God and hard work are the best doctors." Only once, when he caught pneumonia, was John allowed to miss helping at harvest time.

John, being the eldest boy, was expected to work the hardest. The heavy jobs at such a young age stunted his growth. He was the runt of the family, but his muscles were hard, and he could bear great hardship.

The land at Fountain Lake Farm, which had never been good soil to begin with, soon wore out.

"Only five bushels an acre this year," Father complained. "I'm going to look at land over Hickory Hill way."

So, after eight years of backbreaking work, they moved a few miles eastward and began the whole job over again. Worse, there was no water on this farm.

They started digging a well three feet wide. The first ten feet down went smoothly. Then they hit sandstone. Father tried blasting, but he lacked the skill. Finally, he turned the job over to John. "Ye'll use a hammer and chisels. The job must be done."

So John went to work in the cramped hole in the ground. Davie lowered him in the bucket. He worked all day, except for a break at dinner. Chip by chip, day by day, month by month, he sank that well.

One morning as he started to work, John felt dizzy. He began to sway back and forth.

Father noticed that it was quiet, "What is keeping ye from the work then?" he called.

John whispered, "Take me out."

Fathers shout roused him from the dizzy spell, "Get in the basket! Hold on!"

Father and Davie managed to haul him out just as he passed out.

A neighbor, Mr. Duncan, who had been a miner, said that the trouble had been caused by carbonic acid gas. "Many a comrade have I seen dead with choke-damp. None so near death as you, John, and escaped without help. It's God's mercy," he said.

Mr. Duncan taught them how to get air into the well. They struck water at ninety feet down.

The shock of his near death added to John's bitterness toward his father for over-working him. *He never spent an hour in that well!* thought John.

5

The Creatures of God

As he grew older, John became ever more sympathetic toward animals.

Mr. McRath, a Highland Scots neighbor to the Muir's, had made a pet of a raccoon. Since these animals usually hid all day in hollow trees, coons were seldom seen. It was a treat for John to see this pet.

"Coonie, Little Man, how are ye the day?" Mr. McRath would ask.

The coon would begin to search his pockets, "Na, there's naught in my pouch for ye the day."

John would say, "I'll fetch something." Off home he would go for bread, carrots, or a bit of meat. Or he would search the woods for nuts and berries for the little animal.

John would imitate Mr. McRath, "Here ye are, Little Man."

And the coon would feel for his offerings with its small man-like paws.

The gentle Highlander taught John that he could make a pet of a wild animal. "Ye must just be sympathetic and enter a little way into the animal's life."

A less gentle lesson was taught in the matter of the muskrats.

The boys liked to watch these small mammals in the rushy areas 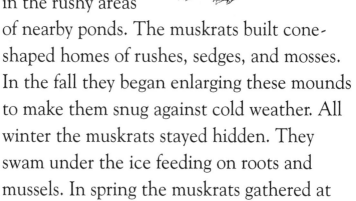 of nearby ponds. The muskrats built cone-shaped homes of rushes, sedges, and mosses. In the fall they began enlarging these mounds to make them snug against cold weather. All winter the muskrats stayed hidden. They swam under the ice feeding on roots and mussels. In spring the muskrats gathered at

spots where the pond ice had melted. They
dived for food, and then they sat on the edge
of the ice nibbling. That is when the hunters
shot them. Sometimes thirty to forty were
taken each day by a single hunter. The hunters could sell the skins for a dime or so. John
felt that it was, "like shooting boys and girls
for their garments."

Perhaps the animal death that he felt the
worst was that of the horse, Nob. Father had
bought the span of work horses, Nob and
Nell. "You're the eldest, so these horses are in
your charge," Father had instructed him.

John found that Nob was fond of him,
and that she was very smart. She became a
family pet. Nob would come running when-
ever John called to her.

One summer
day Mr. Muir
drove Nob to a
church meeting
in Portage. He
seldom missed

any of the religious meetings in the area. It was a hot day, a sandy road, and a long journey of twenty-four miles. When Father returned, John led the exhausted Nob to the stable.

"Father, she's too tired to eat or even lie down," John told him. "She just stands there drooping in her stall."

"She'll be just fine the morn," Father reassured John. But she was not.

"Nob sounds like I did when I had pneumonia," John reported to his father next morning.

Finally alerted, Mr. Muir ordered, "Bathe her head and try to get her to eat something. I'll go for the Methodist."

"Can't we do more than just pray for Nob?" John asked.

Father wasn't a humorous man, but he almost smiled. "Na, the minister's a jack-of-all-trades. A good horse doctor he is."

But the Methodist could not help Nob. For two weeks she trailed feebly after the children. John bathed her head and stroked her. He could not get her to eat. The look in her eyes broke his heart. At last she lay down, gasped her last breath, and died. All the family wept for her.

John did more than sorrow for Nob. He thought deeply about how men treated animals. *Why did Father drive Nob so hard in the heat that she died? Why did the church and school teach that animals had no mind, no soul, no rights? Were not animals and human both creatures of God?*

6

John Begins to Study

When John was about sixteen, he began to wish that his schooling had not ended so early.

"Father," he asked, "will you buy me an arithmetic book?"

"Were you not taught in grammar school then?" Father replied.

"I learned the rules, but did not understand them."

"The Bible is the only book any man must understand in this life," Father said.

"But some science is necessary," John argued. "You could not read your Bible without your spectacles."

"Oh," Father replied, "men more worldly can study optics and make the spectacles."

"But," objected John, quoting from the Bible, "'All shall know the Lord from the least even to the greatest.' Then who will make the spectacles?"

"John, you are over eager to argue," Father scolded. "I will buy the book as long as you promise to keep up with your farm chores."

John studied the arithmetic book. Then he went on to study higher mathematics and other subjects.

John had known most of the Bible by heart at age eleven. Now he read it again to enjoy it as poetry. He also read the poetry of Shakespeare and Milton. He saved every penny and bought books by other poets. From neighbors, he borrowed several dozen books. Among these were novels by Scott. He kept these carefully hidden. Novels were forbidden reading.

Bedtime was right after family worship, about eight o'clock in winter. Each night John tried to steal a few precious minutes to read. After five minutes, Father would catch him. "John, to bed! You must go when the family goes to bed. Why must you be given a separate order each night?"

One night Father told him, "You may get up early in the morning to read if you like. If you **will** read, do it then."

As he went to bed, John thought, *I hope that I can wake up before Father calls me in the morning.* And the clock in his head did wake him up. He tiptoed down to the kitchen and looked at the clock. *One o'clock! Five whole hours, almost half a day to read!*

The house proved to be too cold to sit and read. It was heated only by the fire in the kitchen, which often burned out at night. John thought of all the heat that they had wasted burning the brush in great bonfires. *Father will object about the time it takes to cut firewood if I build up the fire,* he thought. *I'll have to keep moving to stay warm.* He took his candle to the cellar. There he had a few tools which had been brought from Scotland. John made others out of scrap materials. He started working on an invention, a model of a self-setting sawmill.

Every morning, after five hours of sleep, he woke up at one o'clock and started work in the freezing cellar. His workshop was right under his father's bed. He wondered how long it would be before his father objected to the noise. Father's patience lasted two weeks.

After saying grace at supper that night, Father said, "Ahem." As no idle words were ever spoken at table in this stern household, the family knew Father was going to say something important. "John, when are ye getting up the morn?"

"About one o'clock."

"In the middle of the night, and disturbing the family!"

John reminded him, "You said that I could get up as early as I wished."

"I know I did," Father said in a strangled voice, "but in the middle of the night?"

John kept silent. Father believed that a Scotsman must not go back on his word.

John continued his work. He made water wheels, door locks and latches, thermometers, clocks, lamp and fire lighters, and many other unusual devices.

At times Father scolded, "It would be better for ye if ye spent even half as much time studying the way of God a ye spend in this useless nonsense." But most of the time he let John use the inventions around the farm.

John stayed on the farm even after he was of an age to seek a job on his own. He thought, *I should like to be a doctor, but it costs too much. If I could get into a factory, I could earn some money. In a factory I could use what I learned while I was inventing things.*

"John Muir," a friendly neighbor said to him, "you were raised not to be thinking highly of yourself. You're a genius. Take your inventions to the state fair. When people see them, any shop in the country will welcome you."

So John chose two wooden clocks and a thermometer to take to the Wisconsin State Fair at Madison.

7

John's Inventions
Win Him Fame

"Na, I'll not be giving ye money for such foolishness," Father said when John told him about going to Madison. "Ye must depend upon yourself."

John still had the gold coin his grandfather had given him so long ago. He had saved about ten dollars. With this small amount, he left home. Father allowed Davie to drive him to Pardeeville to catch the train. This was only nine miles from Hickory Hill, but John had never been that far away from home before.

Before he left, Father warned him, "John,

you may think I have been hard on ye. Ye will find that strangers are harder still."

John found that just the opposite was true.

The landlord of the Pardeeville Tavern came to the railroad platform to look at John's curious parcel. "What have ye there, young man?"

"A machine for keeping time," John replied, "and another for getting you up in the morning."

"Where'd ye get the patterns?"

"I made the up in my head," said John.

Soon a small crowd gathered to look at the wooden clocks. The tavern keeper explained them as if they were his own inventions. John stood shyly by and listened to the crowd's compliments without being embarrassed.

Next morning the train conductor also took a friendly interest in John's machines. John asked him, "Do you think I might ride on the engine?"

The conductor told the engineer, "This boy has made some strange machines. He wants to see how the train engine works. Let

him ride up here."

So John rode the engine all the way. He felt as if he was flying as the locomotive rushed through the landscape.

When they arrived in Madison, he thanked the conductor and the engineer. They directed him to the fairgrounds. There, he ran into another good-natured fellow. The ticket agent exclaimed, "Well, you've got things to exhibit! **You** don't need a ticket. Take your machines up to the Fine Arts Hall, that big place up on the hill."

A special shelf was built to display John's two clocks and his thermometer. People were loud with their praise. John's display seemed to be the most popular in the show. Even the Eastern newspapers carried a story of the farm

boy's original inventions. John won a prize
and a special diploma. But John was confused
by all the attention. He was afraid to enjoy
the praise. His father had for so long taught
him that praise was evil.

John worked at a few odd jobs, hoping to
earn money to enroll in the state university.
He loved to walk on the lawn of the university grounds. There were many trees and
some beautiful lakes. One day while walking
there, he talked to a student who had seen his
inventions. John told him, "You're a lucky
fellow to be studying here. I haven't enough
money, or I'd join you."

Doesn't take but about a dollar a week for
a freshman to board. Most of us live on bread
and milk. Give it a try."

John went Professor Stirling who was
Acting President of the university at the time.
"I was in grammar school in Scotland until I
was eleven," John told him. "I've studied
higher math at home. I have read a great
many books."

"Tell me what books you have been reading," Professor Stirling asked. After hearing John out, he welcomed him to the university. John was overjoyed.

He earned his own way through four years at the university. In summer, he worked in the fields. In winter, he taught school.

But even with his studies and his work, he found time to tinker on his machines. Some of them were handy, some funny. One fire starter clock had his schoolhouse warmed up before he arrived. John's landlord said, "Humph, it's the schoolhouse you'll be setting afire, young man." John invented a desk which presented him with each book to study for a set time, grabbed it back, and served him up another. One of his clocks dumped him out of bed in the morning. The odd machines made John's room a gathering place for fellow students and even for John's professors.

John did not graduate from the university. He had taken no set course of studies. He chose to study subjects that he felt would be of most use to him. Botany, the study of plants, was the subject above all others which caught his interest.

It wasn't a professor, but a fellow student named Griswold, who gave him his first botany lesson. Handing John a flower from a tall locust tree, Griswold asked, "What plant family does the locust belong to, Muir?"

"I haven't studied botany," John replied, "but it's like the pea flowers from our kitchen garden at home."

"Right! Pea family, even though peas are small vines and the locust tree is immense. The parts of the flowers and leaves are alike. Taste the leaf."

"It **does** taste like a pea," John said.

"God created some things to be alike in all the variety of His universe. Man can study the plant world to see the oneness of The Creator's universe," Griswold told him.

John was charmed. He went on long excursions to gather plants to study. He studied their *inner* beauty. He wanted to understand deeply God's plan for one part of His creation.

8

A Stay in Canada

"But I'm a botanist," John protested to the Mountie.

"Yer a runaway from Her Majesty's Army, and I'm taking ye in. Are ye coming peaceable?"

"Look, Sergeant," John said, "here is my plant press. I've specimens from the forest. See tamarack, heathwort, elm . . . and look at this! A Calypso, a Hider of the North. Have you ever seen a wee bloom so filled with God's spirit? Now if I was a fugitive, do you think I'd be about taking samples of the flora?"

"But the Campbells told me. . . ."

John threw back his head and howled with laughter. "Those Campbell boys! I'm sorry, Sergeant. Bill and Alex were playing a joke on me. I'm living with the Campbells right now. My name is John Muir, and I **am** a botanist."

"And what might a botanist be?" the sergeant asked.

John tried to explain, but to the sergeant, as to most people in those days, the scramble to get their shelter and their daily bread was so hard that they had no thoughts beyond themselves.

"Righto then. Ye may be a little daft," the sergeant said, tapping his forehead, "but I guess yer not our runaway. I'll be about me business."

Due to a lost letter, John had missed a chance to go as a free student for another year at the university. He had worked a while for David Galloway, his brother-in-law, who had bought Fountain Lake Farm from Mr. Muir. Then he had gone botanizing in

Canada. He had stayed with many families, including the fun-loving Campbells.

John wandered the evergreen swamps of Canada making crayon sketches and taking plant samples to study. He was careless of his own comfort and safety. Often he slept in the woods without blankets. A loaf of bread bought from a pioneer farm wife would keep him fed for days of wandering in the beauties of nature.

The evening he had discovered the little Calypso flower, he had been hungry, lost in the swamp, and fearful of having no dry land to sleep on. The discovery of the new bloom excited him so much that it gave him energy to keep going. He finally came to a log house. "Why have ye been in tha' cold, dreary bog then? Many a poor soul has been lost in there and never been

found." The settler shook his head in amazement when

John told him he had been looking for flowers.

Forest and swamp were John's welcome friends. He gloried in storms. Wind blown leaves and chattering brooks preached him sermons. He was at home in his universe.

While at university, John had read Darwin's ideas that the earth and its animals had evolved over many millions of years. He had accepted the idea. Though people even nowadays sometimes argue that it cannot be so because of what the Bible says, John believed that both accounts were true. He figured they just told the same story in different ways.

John's gentle mother sent him pressed flowers and wrote to tell him to take care of his health and keep his faith in God. His father's letters showed that he regarded John's explorations as almost sinful. The strongest support for his studies came in the letters from Mrs. Jeanne Carr, another botanist.

John had met Jeanne Carr, wife of Professor Ezra Slocum Carr, at the state fair where he had displayed his clocks. He felt them to be fellow students, but at very different levels. Mrs. Carr had studied and loved the science of botany for many years.

John's studies came to an end because he ran out of money. For a year and a half, he was employed in a factory near Georgian Bay. The factory turned out rake, broom, and pitchfork handles. John had entered into an agreement with Mr. Trout, the factory owner. John would work to make the machines in the factory more automatic. He would get half the profit on the improvement in sales.

By March of 1866, they had thirty thousand handles stored for seasoning the wood. During a lightning storm, the factory burned down. Insurance was not common in those days, so the factory was a complete loss.

John trusted the Trout family to repay him when they could. They exchanged letters for years, and finally Mr. Trout did manage to pay all of the debt to John.

John started wandering again. His ability with machines took him to the cities. His heart longed for the countryside.

9

From Indiana to the Atlantic Ocean

John studied his maps. His choice should be a factory town in the Midwest. Then he could study the plants in the deciduous forests of Indiana, as well as the prairie plants of Illinois. And there it was! The city was Indianapolis.

John found work in a carriage factory. He at once began to improve the machinery. One day his boss asked him, "Can we count on you staying with us? We'd like to offer you a job as foreman, and if that proves out, a partnership."

"I'm sorry, sir," John said. "I really am only interested in earning a few hundred dollars. I want to go on with my botany studies."

John's job ended sooner than he had expected. In a mill accident, a file pierced his right eye. The eye liquid seeped out, and his sight faded. Because of shock, the vision in his left eye went also. John was in a panic. He felt he would never again see the wonders of nature.

Friends took John to the eye doctor. "Three to four months in a dark room, young man," the doctor ordered. "I'm sure your sight will be restored, but it may not be just as it was before."

During his time in the dark room, other friends read to John. They also brought to him the flowers that he loved.

John could not live outwardly at this time, so he came closer to his inner thoughts. *Life is short,* he thought. *Why should I spend it in a carriage factory? I'm going to see God's tropic gardens. Florida, Cuba, maybe the Amazon. I will! I will spend the rest of my days studying God's world.*

The injury to his eye was not as serious as he had feared. But he did not go back to the carriage factory. He went home to Wisconsin to say good-bye to his family and friends. He had decided to walk from Indiana to the Gulf of Mexico. He would keep a journal about the plants in each place, and a bit about the people whom he met.

Before he left Fountain Lake Farm, John told his brother-in-law, "Dave, I'd like to buy those forty meadow acres near the lake from you. I'm willing to pay for the fencing. We should preserve some of the wild prairie flowers and grasses before they are gone forever."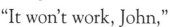

"It won't work, John," David said. "That's just a sentimental dream. Fences never last. Cattle get in."

And so John lost in his first attempt to preserve some of the wilderness.

John returned to Indianapolis where he said good-bye to the friends who had helped him in the dark days. He took a train to Jeffersonville, crossed the Ohio River next morning and started south through Kentucky. He walked about 25 miles a day, carrying only his plant press and one small bag.

In his journal, he wrote, "Miles of hills and untouched forests. Oaks excel any I have ever seen. All the streams taste salty. Groves of giant sunflowers. Mistletoe in trees. Opened my eyes this morning to see two flowers unknown to me. Great cave with fern at the mouth that I would expect to see in the cool of Wisconsin. In summer, folks here sit at the entrance. Always a stream of cool air from the cave mouth."

The Cumberlands were the first mountains John had ever seen. He had been used to walking the shallow hills of the Midwest. Here he met one long up-grade that took more than six hours to climb. He found heathwort, cinnamon fern, and vines loaded with fragrant, yellow flowers. He played with the little ferns called sensitive plants. He wondered if plants had hopes and fears, as he watched the fronds fold and droop at the touch of his hand.

John liked to sleep in the clean forest, but sometimes he did stay overnight with a farm family. One night he stayed with a blacksmith who warned him, "Houses on your path all in ruins since the war. Still dangerous men hiding in the woods. Better turn back."

John did meet some mounted men. "Howdy," he said and walked rapidly on his way. He knew that they were discussing him. *Take me for an herb doctor, with all these plants hanging from the press,* he thought. At any rate, they let him pass.

Of the Tennessee and North Carolina mountain people, John wrote in his journal, "Wear coonskin caps. Brag about their backward machines as if they were very advanced. Women hand-spinning and weaving in every cabin. Some men fighting blood feuds and cannot settle down to work, eat, or sleep. Even the women smoke tobacco."

Once over the Cumberlands, he came to dark pine woods. He saw holly plants for the first time.

Of Georgia, John wrote in his journal, "Cotton fields and piney woods. Tall, cane-like grasses. Long leafed pines 60-70 feet high. Apricot vines, delicious fruit. Pomegranates grown here. Cypress swamps. Trees droop with Spanish moss, like long, gray, grandfather beards. Reached Savannah and the sea. No family will accept me. Too many strangers after the war. No work or money from home. Feel lonesome and poor."

10

Florida, Cuba, and a Surprise Decision

Most people would not choose a grave-yard for a camping spot, but John did. In it he was safe from the roving bands of Negroes who had been freed after the war. John knew the friendly ghosts of the graveyard would protect him from folks who were afraid of spooks.

He built a little hut of bushes and roofed it with moss. An immense live oak tree draped with Spanish moss sheltered his little camp. At first the birds and squirrels scolded him. Then they became his friends. Only the beetles and mosquitoes disturbed him. Living among the dead did not bother him. He wrote in his journal that it was a shame that children were taught that death is a punishment. He felt that nature showed death to be as beautiful as life.

John lived for almost a week in the little hut. He was dizzy from hunger. No work was to be found. In despair, he went once again to the post office.

"Yes, there is a letter for a Mr. Muir. But how do I know **you** are Mr. Muir?" the clerk asked him.

"I have a letter from my brother. Look it over," John said.

"You could have stolen the letter. I need some other proof."

John thought a bit, "My brother's letter says I am a botanist. I might have stolen the letter, but I couldn't steal a knowledge of plants. Ask me anything you wish about the plant world."

The clerk explained the problem to the manager who laughed and said, "Let him have his money."

John went off to buy a meal. He also bought passage on a ship, the Sylvan Shore, bound for Florida.

On the way south, the ship hugged the coastline close to an impassable swamp. Barrier reefs protected the ship from the Atlantic's waves. Nearing their harbor, they sailed through black-water lagoons. John saw

alligators, wading birds, and clumps of mangrove trees. He had reached the Land of Flowers, Florida.

The salt marsh did not match his dream of Florida. The only way west was on a path that had been cut for a railroad. As soon as he left the path, he was in deep water and tangled in vines. A splash might mean a wading bird. Or an Alligator! He thought, *No doubt even alli-*

gators, though cruel and ugly, have their place in God's kingdom. But, even so, he was not eager to meet one.

Yet it was not an alligator which harmed him. Somewhere on his journey, a mosquito carrying malaria germs bit John.

When John had crossed Florida to the Gulf of Mexico, he asked at a small shop about work and about ship passage to Cuba.

"Y'all go 'bout two mile out a town. Ask fer Mr. Hodgson at the lumber mill," said the shopkeeper. "As to Cuba, I dunno."

Mr. Hodgson hired him. "You're very welcome if you can work with machines," Mr. Hodgson told him, and there's a schooner will be coming in two weeks. Takes lumber to Texas. You can easily get a ship from there to Cuba."

Next day John fell ill with fever. He could not eat, but he felt he had to have lemons. He walked back to the little shop to buy them. On the way back, he blacked out. Finally, he crawled and staggered back to the mill. He crawled up the stairs and fell into bed.

Many days later he came awake to hear, "Mary, keep him drinking quinine water. It's all that can be done about malaria." For three months the kindly Hodgsons had nursed him. He owed them his life.

Again, as when he had been blinded, John had time to listen to his inner thoughts. And something new occurred to him, *We are taught that God made the world for man. I don't believe that it is true. Perhaps God made the plants and animals each for their own happiness. Even the little mosquito who fed on me was only seeking food. Why should man feel himself more*

important than each smallest part of creation? We are all part of one universe.

When he was almost well, John sailed on the Island Belle for Cuba. They docked at Havana harbor. Ashore John saw what seemed a golden city because of its yellow homes and yellow flowers.

In Cuba John ate oranges, bananas, and a strange fruit called pineapple. Everywhere there was the noise of voices babbling in a strange language and  the ringing of bells from Morro Castle. He wished he could climb the mountains, but the fever returned. So he studied the palms and the spiny plants like Spanish bayonet which the people used for fences. He thought the gardens to be like fairyland.

After a month in Cuba, John began to look for a ship to South America. He wanted to float down the great Amazon River and study the tropical plants. He had less than $100; his fever was not cured; the Amazon was an unhealthy place. None of these sensible reasons for **not** going stopped him. He was saved because he could not find a ship.

One day he was resting in a public garden while reading a newspaper. In it he saw an ad for a ship going to another place he wished to visit. He made a surprising decision.

11

John Chooses California

John traveled on a small ship which carried oranges to New York. From there he could catch a ship for Panama.

The crew were friendly to John, though perhaps they could not quite share his enchantment with the sea. "I would like to ramble on the hills of the waves, sleep on a bed of foam and salty seaweed," he told the sailors. They thought him a little crazy, but they listened to him, wide-eyed.

John lived on the "orange ship" while it was docked in New York. His health improved with the cold weather. Finally, he found a ship sailing to Panama.

The low-paying passengers were crammed into the ship. Tempers ran high and fights were frequent, especially at mealtime. John wrote of the glorious tropic flowers that he saw, but he preferred to forget that unpleasant voyage.

It was April of 1868, when the ship from Panama to San Francisco landed its passengers. John had had enough of humans. He was ready for the wilderness.

It had been twenty years since that first gold nugget, discovered at Sutter's Mill, had started the Gold Rush. People still flocked to California to get rich quick. But John was looking for another kind of gold.

On Main Street he stopped a man to ask, "How do I find my way out of this town?"

"Where do you want to go?" the man asked John.

"I'm looking for any place wild," John replied.

The man gave John an odd look, pointed toward the Oakland Ferry, and hurried away glancing nervously over his shoulder.

John crossed the bay on the ferry. He walked over the low Coast Range. There  before him was the gold he was seeking. The Great Central Valley was golden with buttercups. Meadow larks sang to him as he walked east toward the mountains.

And there they were, peak upon peak, the mountains he later called The Range of Light. Like a rainbow, their colors shaded from red-purple at the base, then blue-purple forests, up to pearly-gray snow-capped crowns.

John traveled the Sierra Mountains with a wandering Englishman.

They thought the Yosemite Canyon a wonder beyond marvels. John became determined to spend as many years there as he could manage. But he would first have to earn some money.

In those first years, he worked breaking horses. He ran a ferry. He sheared sheep and herded sheep. He enjoyed his job as a shepherd because it gave him time to study the plants and animals of the Sierra.

A man who had noticed John's love of plants, offered John a job. "My sheep have to be moved up into the Yosemite, Mr. Muir. If you will keep an eye on my lazy shepherd, I'll transport your plant press and your gear and see to it that there is food at each camp. You would have to help if bears attacked the sheep. Will you do it?"

John was delighted. They spent six weeks in the Yosemite Valley. Later, when bears **did** attack the sheep, the camp was moved into the high grassy meadows. John climbed mountains, sketched new plants, wrote notes, and traced the paths of glaciers which had melted long before. His only worry was that the sheep, which he called "four-footed locusts," would destroy the wilderness with their close grazing of the plants.

In a letter to his sister Sarah, John described the Yosemite:

> The Merced River, called the River of Mercy, lies in a valley at four thousand feet. The main valley is seven miles long and a half mile wide. The valley sides are granite that is cut sheer, as if a giant had sliced them with a knife. The valley is like a great hall lit by the sky. The rock faces were polished by ancient glaciers.

Other valleys join the main Yosemite, but they end high above the level of the main valley. From each, a waterfall cascades into the Merced. The sun and spray form rainbows, and the walls by each falls are a fernery kept green by mist.

Knowing how you love all nature, I wish that you could see Yosemite, dear Sarah.

John decided to stay in Yosemite. At first he stayed in a hotel built by a Mr. Hutchins for the visitors to Yosemite. Later, he built a cabin for himself while working for Mr. Hutchins in the building of a sawmill.

John never did things in an ordinary way. He dug a ditch in the floor of his cabin to let a stream of water flow through. The floor slabs were spaced so that ferns could grow up between them. His bed was suspended from the ceiling. The gurgle of water sang him to sleep.

At this time, Professor Carr was appointed to a position at the University of California. When the Carrs moved to Oakland, they invited John to visit them, but he wanted to study the mountains in wintertime. Letters carried in and out of the valley by Indian Tom were his only contact with those he loved.

John sent Mrs. Carr his plant specimens to care for. She sent him books, which he read in the evenings by his fireside. The ideas he read in the books of the scientists, Lyell and Darwin, made him think deeply. *They say that the world's mountains, even its animals, were shaped over centuries. Then why should it be true that the Yosemite was shaped in one great disaster?* he asked himself.

Most of John's friends tried to get him away from the mountains for his own safety. Even Mrs. Carr, who usually understood him, did not want to hear about the storms and cold, and his dangerous exploring. Only the great thinker, Emerson, said to him, "When you have lived alone enough and studied enough, John, then you will tell the world of what you have learned."

John stayed in the mountains.

12

What Formed Yosemite Valley?

John watched as the dark rainbow colors danced in the mist of the falls. At this time of night the arc of color stretched from the top of Yosemite Falls straight down to the white foam below the falls.

I wonder how the moon would look if I could see it through the water, John thought. He edged out onto Fern Ledge. He saw the moon's light shimmer as he viewed it from behind the falling water. The music of the falls pounded in his ears. Suddenly the wind shifted the column of water. It felt to John as if great stones were striking his shoulders. He dropped to his knees and curled up. His life depended upon the wind. Would the water sway away or come closer? At last another wind shift freed him. He crept along the ledge by the fall's icy wall. Drenched and numb with cold, he hurriedly climbed down the fourteen hundred foot cliff and went home to warm himself at his fireside. The adventure excited him; the danger, he forgot.

John was not careless, but he never let comfort get in the way of his explorations. He climbed five hundred foot ice cones below the valley's falls in winter using an ice ax to cut steps.

One winter day he climbed four hundred feet in snow up to his waist. As he crossed the head of a canyon, the soft snow started to slide. John rode the avalanche as it swished and roared to the foot of the canyon. What a thrill!

He climbed eight thousand feet to the Sierra mountain peaks in winter to study snow banners. These wavy, silken flags of snow streamed from each Sierra peak when the snow was dry and the north wind blew.

The Inyo earthquake of 1872 made Yosemite's cliffs and domes tremble like Jello. The Indians and the white settlers trembled, too. Again, John was not afraid; his intent always was to learn. He rushed out of his cabin. The ground rippled, so that he had to balance as if he were walking on the sea.

The Yosemite storekeeper decided to leave. He had always argued with John. "The reason this valley's so deep 'cause the bottom just plumb fell out'n it." He was afraid that an earthquake might prove him right.

John teased him, "Come now, Mother Nature's just joggling us on her knee to amuse us."

The storekeeper was too frightened to enjoy the joke. "You take my key, John. I'm leaving."

"You'll never have another chance to have so grand a burial," John joked.

But the man was not to be persuaded.

There was reason to be afraid. Eagle Rock had fallen fifteen hundred feet to the valley floor. Other boulders had also crashed down the cliffs. The earthquake was found to have registered 8.25 on the Richter Scale, a great earthquake. But John thought about the one which three centuries before had sent house sized boulders crashing down. Compared with that time, this had been a small quake.

John saw the beauty of the mountains with the eye of a poet. But in his studies of the landforms, he thought as a scientist. He had found proof that the whole mountain range, almost to the highest peaks, had been covered by five giant glaciers. Everywhere, he found boulders which had been carried by glaciers far away from where they had formed. He found round glacier-formed lakes. Rock walls were scratched where stones frozen into the ice had raked them as the glacier flowed by. Some rock faces were so highly polished by the glacier that he could climb them only

with bare feet. At one spot an ice-river had
flowed uphill for over five hundred feet. No
river of water could erode rocks in such a
way.

John wrote to his Mother:

> I know how Yosemite, and all these
> great valleys, were formed. I am going to
> spend the next years writing their history.
>
> Mother, the proof is plain to see for
> anyone who doesn't wear blinders on his
> mind. As snowflakes fell year by year, they
> were crushed into giant glaciers. All but the
> very highest peaks were smothered in an ice-
> blanket. Whenever two or more glaciers
> flowed together, they caused the rock domes
> to break. The smooth faces of these cut

> mountains line the
> valleys.
>
> I wish you could see
> Half Dome. It rises
> forty-eight hundred feet
> from the valley floor.
> The upper half is almost
> straight up. At the base

of the cliff are slabs of rock which were split off from the face like slices from a round loaf of bread.

Mother, do not worry about me so. I am never lost in the wilderness. God guides me. He keeps me safe from danger. He shows me all His truths.

Bless you for the flowers. They brought to my mind the springtime at Fountain Lake.

13

John Begins to Write

To Mrs. Carr, John wrote:

Friends are pushing me to write my ideas for the magazines. I'm tempted. I'm afraid, though, that my studies would suffer from it.

Mrs. Carr encouraged John to write. She took care of his plant samples. She rewrote his scribbled notebooks. She sent some of his papers East to Emerson to get them published. Many scientists and artists came to the Yosemite Valley to have John guide them through the mountains. Often it was

Mr. Carr who had sent them to John. These people, too, urged John to publish his ideas about the Yosemite.

Finally, John was persuaded. He sent an article titled "Yosemite Glaciers" to *The New York Daily Tribune*. It appeared in the paper in 1871. It was the first time that John had made a public statement about how he thought Yosemite Valley had been formed. It was not long before he heard what others thought.

Geologist Josiah Dwight Whitney was a professor at Harvard University. He was known as a leading scientist in both America and Europe. Professor Whitney had written a geology of California and guidebooks to Yosemite. In them he had stated that an up-heaval of the Sierra Mountain chain had caused the floor of the Yosemite Valley to sink. Whitney was furious that a young man with little education and training in geology should question his ideas.

When John guided the minister, Dr. Joseph Cook, up to Cloud's Rest, the minister lectured him. "Look at the wonders spread before you. Surely the hand of God created them just as they are now. How can you truly believe that they have been changed by ice."

John's father wrote him:

> You are cheating God. Burn your papers, so that your ideas will not harm you or others. Turn your thoughts to God.

John was young, only thirty. He had not graduated from a university. He had studied only the small bit of geology that a new, unimportant university in the Midwest could give him. But he knew what his eyes had observed.

By 1873, John was sending about one article a month to Mrs. Carr. She sent them to *Overland Monthly*. The readers enjoyed John's articles. He wrote clearly, as a scientist would. His writing was also touched by his poet's eye.

John lived in the city of Oakland for ten months while he wrote. *The Overland Monthly* paid him well for his writing. But he did not like the hard, lonely work. Mountains and glaciers of continents he had not yet seen filled his daydreams. His health always suffered when he had to stay indoors. Soon he felt that he must return to the mountains.

Many of the mountain people had read John's articles. They welcomed him back. But John felt that a period of his life was over; that he must move on. Yet he found it hard to leave. He visited all his favorite places to say good-bye for a while. He intended to travel the wild places and write about what he observed.

John traveled from Mt. Shasta, in northern California, south through the Sierras to Yosemite. For five months he explored, writing in his journal of the people, the animals, and the plants that he met. Each adventure was later written into an article for the newspapers.

Near Shasta, a man asked John, "Where are you headed so late in the season?"

John told him, "Going to Shasta."

"Shasta City?"

"Oh, no," replied John. "I'm going to climb Mt. Shasta."

"You're late by two months to climb Shasta," the man protested. "You'll freeze to death."

"But I like snow and ice," John said. "I'm used to climbing in it." And **go** he did.

John was at the nine thousand foot level when he was caught in a storm. He had seen the storm coming. He had gathered wood and built a snow shelter. For five days John was snug in his hidey-hole while the storm raged around him. He made friends with the wild sheep which sheltered near his camp. On the sixth day, he was "rescued" by his worried friends. He did not want to leave the mountain. Notes from this adventure were written into his article "*Wild Wool*."

On his way back south, John came upon a storm near Yuba City. He climbed an immense Douglas fir tree to enjoy the storm. From this experience, he wrote "*A Windstorm in the Forests of the Yuba*," a favorite with his readers.

In the five months of this trip, John came to a new understanding of how important it was for man to live with nature. "City men are mean-spirited and greedy," he wrote. "They lose sight of the better part of themselves and of the beauty of the world. Country dwellers are little better. Often, they too, just count the sheep or the bushels of grain that they can take from nature. Every man needs the woods to keep in touch with his soul."

People all across the country were reading John's articles. In a small way, he was keeping people in touch with nature.

14

John Speaks for the Forests

John walked
the Sequoia
forest which
stretched one
hundred eighty
miles along the
west slopes of
the Sierras. He

found five sawmills operating in the Big Tree
belt. These trees were so huge that the lum-
bermen were blasting them down with dyna-
mite. Much of the lumber in each tree was
blown to splinters.

He passed by areas being used for sheep
grazing which were totally bare. The

sheepmen had burned the vegetation to make pastures for their sheep. This had killed all the young trees.

In Tuolumne Valley, he saw a deep gash in the canyon wall. A mining company was washing away the rocks. The damage they were doing to get a tiny amount of gold sickened John.

Hoping to slow this destruction, John wrote a newspaper article. It was a message to alert California lawmakers to these problems. He told them how forest conservation affected the climate, the soil, and the flow of water in the streams. John asked that a survey of the forests be made, so that the government could make sensible laws about the use of forests. The lawmakers did not pay much attention to him. But the people did.

John continued his explorations and his studies. He went on an expedition to Utah. He studied the Redwood forests of northern California. He floated down the Sacramento River.

Sometimes John rented a room in San Francisco. Here he put his notes in order and wrote them up. He liked the privacy to write, but he did not like the solitude. Between his writing times and his exploring journeys, he stayed for longer periods with one family or another. He had always thought of himself as a home-loving man. But here he was, middle-aged, and he had never had a home of his own, nor, some would say, a proper job.

When John had been a three-year-old, Grandfather Gilrye had taken him to see Lord Lauderdale's gardens. The blaze of flowers had dazzled young Johnny's eyes. "Will I ever be rich enough to have flowers like these?" he had asked.

"Sure and you dinna have to be rich, Johnny," the laird's gardener had answered him. "It's just you must be having the green thumb."

Johnny had looked down at his little white thumb.

"You're not understanding, Johnny," Grandfather had said. "He's meaning you must have the knack of growing things."

Johnny had thought that might be a good knack to have, especially after he was treated to a big, red apple from the orchard. He had wished that he might have a green thumb when he grew up. Then he could grow apples and flowers of his very own.

When John was in his forties, his wishes for a home and gardens came true. It came about because friends introduced John to Dr. John Strentzel. Dr. Strentzel had been trained in Europe to grow grapevines and also as a doctor. He had come to America in 1840. He had brought his wife, Louisiana, and his baby girl west to settle in the Alhambra Valley in California. He had become very successful in growing grapevines and fruit orchards.

John was often a guest at the Strentzel's ranch. He was charmed by their daughter, Miss Louie Wanda. But it took more than a pretty face to turn John's head. Louie was educated, she was an outstanding pianist, and she, too, was fond of flowers.

John was busy in San Francisco with writing and lecturing, but he took time out to go courting. When the orchards were in blossom, John and Louie became secretly engaged. They agreed to marry when John returned from a trip to Alaska.

In 1880, they married and moved into the old Strentzel house.

Hidden in the coastal hills, the house had wide verandas draped with roses and ivy. Standing there, they could view the land which John had bought or rented from Dr. Strentzel.

John became a successful fruit farmer. In this, Louie was immensely helpful. Dr. Strentzel had not been in good health. He had depended on Louie to help manage the ranch. She had kept accounts, paid the hired hands, bought supplies, and sold the crops. She had the knowledge of botany needed for successful fruit growing.

Yet Louie was not an outdoor girl. When John took her to show her his Yosemite, she thought there might be a bear behind every tree. She understood, though, that John needed to be often in the mountains and forests. His health always suffered when he was not outdoors. So they agreed that he would continue to travel when times were slow at the ranch.

In the following years, Louie stayed at the ranch and raised their two daughters. John traveled and wrote. He wrote home often, sending his articles for Louie's approval.

John received $100 to $250 for every article that he wrote, a good sum at that time. At the end of ten years, they were wealthy enough to sell the land, so that John could spend all his time traveling and writing.

John traveled to five continents to study the forests. He helped to start the Sierra Club and was its president until his death. This was formed as a mountain climbing club, but its main purpose was to protect the wilderness.

John guided President Theodore Roosevelt and other important men through the mountains and persuaded them to pass laws to save the trees.

John wrote many articles and books to tell people about the wonders of the western wilderness. He wrote that everyone must be responsible for saving this beauty. He told people that the forests were not created just for man's use. For twenty-four years, John spoke for the forests.

John Made His Mark on History

The leaders, as well as the people of the United States, were inspired by John Muir's many letters, articles, and books. Many millions of acres of forest and range lands were set aside and protected from development by Presidents Harrison, Cleveland, and Theodore Roosevelt.

From 1889-1890, John Muir, in cooperation with the magazine editor Robert Underwood Johnson, wrote articles to awaken public interest in creating a Yosemite National Park. Johnson used these articles to urge the Committee on Public Lands to press

Congress to set up a park within the boundaries proposed by Muir. In 1890, Yosemite
National Park was created. That same year a
wave of public interest also helped to push
through bills to create Sequoia and General
Grant National Parks.

Muir suggested that the King's Canyon
area be included in Sequoia Park. The bill
was defeated in Congress, but John W. Noble,
then the Secretary of the Interior, had been
inspired by Muir. He wrote a law to let presidents just proclaim lands to be set aside for
forest reserves. In 1893, using this bill, President Harrison protected thirteen million
acres. King's Canyon was finally made a park
in 1940.

In 1905, Muir discovered and named the
"Blue Forest" section of the Petrified Forest.
He urged President Theodore Roosevelt to
set it aside as a national monument.

A butterfly, a plant, and even a station on
the Santa Fe Railroad, were named in honor
of John Muir. Colleges granted him honorary

degrees. California recognized his lifetime achievements by naming a John Muir Day to be celebrated in all schools. Glaciers, mountains, and other geographical features bear his name to this day. But the honor which was closest to his heart was a park created in 1908 to protect about five hundred acres of his beloved coast redwood trees. The donors, Mr. and Mrs. William Kent, named it Muir Woods National Monument in his honor.

Muir's Sierra Club today has a leading part in the ongoing campaign to preserve and even to restore such places in the wilderness as the Hetch Hetchy.

By the time John Muir died in 1914, his dream of protecting the wilderness had greatly enriched the lives of the American people. He had made a difference in his world.

JOHN MUIR

photo provided by the National Park Service

California

From 1889-1890, John Muir, in cooperation with magazine editor Robert Underwood Johnson, wrote articles to awaken public interest in creating a Yosemite National Park. Johnson used these articles to urge the Committee on Public Lands to press Congress to set up a park within the boundaries proposed by Muir. In 1890, Yosemite National Park was created. That same year the wave of public interest also helped to push through bills to create Sequoia and General Grant National Parks.

In Muir Woods National Monument the lartest redwood was 246 ft. tall, 17 ft. thick through the trunk, and had been growing since the time that Christ was on the earth.

Muir Woods
Muir Beach
John Muir Parkway
Martinez, site of the old Strentzel house, preserved as it was when Muir lived and worked in it from 1890-1914.

King's Canyon National Park
General Grant National Park
Muir Grove Big Trees
Sequoia National Park

Yosemite National Park
Muir Gorge on the Lyell Fork of Tuolomne River
John Muir Trail
John Muir Wilderness
Mount Muir, 14,015 ft.

In 1871, Muir discovered living glaciers in the Sierra Mountains. He crawled into a crevasse, a deep crack in the glacier, and found walls of clear green ice. He planted stakes across the face of the glacier and measured the progress of the flowing ice at one inch each day. He spotted dozens of other living glaciers which could be seen from the summit of Mt. Lyell.

Muir suggested that King's Canyon area be included in Sequoia Park. The bill was defeated in Congress, but John W. Noble, then the Secretary of the Interior had been inspired by Muir. He wrote a law to let presidents just proclaim lands to be set aside for forest reserves. Using this bill in 1893, President Harrison protected 13 million acres.

94

While collecting plants on the arctic tundra at
Wrangell Island, John Muir found a new species of
erigeron. He sent the plant to botanist Asa Gray of
Harvard University. Dr. Gray named it Ivesia Muirii
in Muir's honor.

Russia

Alaska

Canada

Mount Muir in the
Chugach Mountains.
7,605 ft.

Muir Glacier in the
St. Elias Mountains

Muir Inlet of
Glacier Bay

Muir Point

In 1879, Muir discovered Glacier Bay
and a number of enormous glaciers
above the bay. One glacier is named for
him. He discovered other glaciers
above Holkham and Taylor Bays.

PATRICIA TOPP, a resident of Michigan, received an M.A. in Education from Wayne State University and was a grade school teacher for 32 years, as well as a tutor for adult illiterates. Continuing to develop her skills after retirement, she has also written *Stepping Off Life's Sad Merry-Go-Round: Metaphorically Speaking* and *This Strange Quantum World and You,* as well as numerous articles and poetry. As a counselor, she is certified in Clinical Hypnotherapy, Imperative Self Analysis, and Neuro-Linguistic Programming.

Also by Patricia Topp
This Strange Quantum World and You

ISBN: 1-57733-035-8, paperback, 64 pages, 17 illustrations, $8.95

This Strange Quantum World and You is a book for those from 9 to 90 who wish to gain some understanding of this quantum world. This smaller-than-an-atom world can't be seen, but there are ways to gain insight into its workings.

This book is geared toward children and provides a few simple experiments to explain how energy and matter work. It also shows how energy and matter are two different states of the same thing. Learning how information is carried at speeds faster than light suggests the conclusion that we are connected in some way. This leads children to a feeling of belonging. It also illustrates the necessity of watching how we think, speak, and act, so that we do a more responsible job of caring for our Earth and for each other.

The book ends with the American Indian tale of Grandmother Spider who spins the web which holds the universe together and ties us all into the universe of the ONE.

"Patricia Topp has done a remarkable job of translating the language of quantum physics into one that a child can understand."

—Fritjof Capra, author of *The Tao of Physics*

LEWELLING SCHOOL
5325 S.E. Logus Road
Milwaukie, Oregon 97222

Made in the USA
Charleston, SC
03 January 2011